Why Go to Confession?

by
Fr. John Flader

All booklets are published thanks to the generous support of the members of the Catholic Truth Society

Contents

A gift from Christ

Some years ago when I was chaplain in a university residential college, a student who had recently returned to the practice of confession after a long time, came to me and said: "Father, please pray for a friend of mine. We are going away on a study weekend, and I am trying to get him to go to confession during this time. I told him that if he goes, I personally will do 500 times the penance the priest gives him." Needless to say, I was astounded and we quickly calculated how long it would take him to say 500 Rosaries, in case the confessor proposed a generous penance! When I caught up with the student again in the middle of the following week I asked him how it had gone with his friend. He said, with an obvious look of joy on his face, that he was doing 100 times the penance. Intrigued, I asked him what had happened. "The offer of 500 was only valid for the weekend", he said with a smile, "but he went to confession today." When I asked him what the penance had been, he answered with a look of relief: "an act of thanksgiving".

I relate this anecdote because it highlights both the great joy experienced when someone goes back to confession after a long time and the resulting eagerness to share that joy with others by encouraging them to go as well. Today, that joy is experienced by too few, as far fewer people go to confession than was the case 50 years ago. The long queues of people waiting to confess their sins in years gone by, are today to be found in few churches. So much is this the case that Pope John Paul II, in his Apostolic Exhortation *Reconciliatio et paenitentia* in 1984, bluntly stated that "the Sacrament of Penance is in crisis."

Great treasure

This situation is most unfortunate, because, in my opinion, the Sacrament of Reconciliation is one of the greatest treasures of the Catholic Church. It is a gift from Jesus Christ, indeed his first gift to the Church after the resurrection. On the afternoon of that first Easter, when he appeared to the Apostles in the Upper Room "he breathed on them, and said to them, 'Receive the Holy Spirit; when you forgive men's sins, they are forgiven, when you hold them bound, they are held bound'." (*Jn* 20:22-23) If Jesus himself has given us this gift we would be most ungrateful and even foolish if we did not make use of it. Having heard many thousands of confessions over the years, I can attest to the fact that the ministry of the confessional is one of the greatest blessings for the priest as well as for the penitent. It is a forum in which one experiences the grace of God acting in a gentle yet powerful way, always leaving the penitent with a great peace and joy.

Why did Christ institute a sacrament for the forgiveness of sins?

People who find it difficult to go to confession and non-Catholics often ask: "Why do we have to go to confession?" Why did Jesus Christ institute a sacrament – an outward sign which confers grace – for the forgiveness of sins if it only makes life more difficult for us? Why can't we simply go straight to God in heaven, telling him we are sorry and be forgiven? As it is, we have to seek out a priest, perhaps wait in a queue or find that the priest isn't even there, or discover that we don't like the priest anyway, and then confess our sins, all of which can be troublesome. Surely it would have been easier if we could just confess directly to God.

The answer must surely be that Our Lord instituted a sacrament for the forgiveness of sins because he knew human nature and he knew we needed it. After all he was the Son of Man. He knew us, and he knew that it would be a great help for us to receive forgiveness through the mediation of a priest. Why? I would say for four reasons.

1. We all sin

Firstly, there is the fact that we all sin. In spite of our efforts to do good, we still commit sins, whether venial sins such as impatience, angry remarks, or gossip; or mortal sins like missing Mass on Sunday through our own fault, impure acts or drunkenness. St John reminds us that "if we say we have no sin, we deceive ourselves, and the truth is not in us." (1 *Jn* 8:11) And Jesus himself teaches us to pray: "Forgive us our trespasses." (*Mt* 6:12)

What can happen, though, is that we lose the sense of sin, the awareness of our sinfulness before God. Cardinal Silvio Oddi, the then Prefect of the Sacred Congregation for the Clergy, said in Philadelphia in 1982: "It would be consoling to be able to maintain that there are now more Communions and fewer confessions because fewer sins are being committed. The headlines of the daily papers, however, do not permit us to be satisfied with that explanation. What has happened, of course, is that the people's *sense of sin* has been eroded systematically."

Pope Pius XII summed it up graphically in a radio message in 1946: "The sin of the century is the loss of the sense of sin."

There is no doubt that the practice of confession, with the examination of conscience which precedes it, is an excellent way of keeping alive and growing in the awareness of our sinfulness. Pope Benedict XVI said in an address to confessors on 19th February 2007: "On experiencing the Lord's tenderness and forgiveness, the penitent more easily acknowledges the gravity of sin and reinforces his decision to avoid it and to remain and grow in his renewed friendship with him." One could add that confession also affords the opportunity of clearing up doubts about what is and what is not sin, and about which sins are venial and which are mortal.

2. We have a need to apologise

A second aspect of human nature which points to the helpfulness of confession is the deep human need to apologise when we have offended someone. If a man inadvertently forgets to kiss his wife goodbye as he usually does on leaving the house, and he suddenly remembers on his way to work that he has forgotten, he doesn't merely feel sorry. He picks up the phone as soon as he arrives at work, rings his wife and apologises. He needs and wants to tell her that he is sorry. Only then does he feel at peace. Jesus Christ knew this human need and he gave us in confession a forum in which we can tell him, through the mediation of a human being, "I am sorry". If we have a deep-seated need to tell others we are sorry when we have hurt them, how much more do we need to tell our Father God that we are sorry.

3. We need to tell others what we have done

A third aspect of human nature suggesting the need for confession is the human need to tell others what we have done, including our misdeeds. If we have a car accident, for example, we feel the need to tell someone as soon as possible. Or if we have had an argument with a loved one, we also have a need to tell someone about it. Criminals tell others what they have done, even to boast about it, and sometimes this leads to their arrest. We all share our experiences with our friends at work or over a beer or a cup of coffee. And we do this, even though sometimes we receive bad advice from them or they in turn pass on to others what we have said.

In confession, on the contrary, when we tell the priest what we have done we receive only good advice and the priest is bound by the seal of confession never to reveal our sins to anyone.

I once witnessed in a particularly graphic way how deep the need is to tell others what we have done. A non-Catholic woman told me that some twenty years before she had done something which she knew to be very wrong, but in all those years she had never told anyone about it. The years passed and finally she got up the courage to go to a Catholic Church, where she entered the confessional and told the priest, to her overwhelming relief. Of course the priest couldn't absolve her, but he did give her a blessing. That conversation engraved on my mind in an indelible way the treasure of the Sacrament of Penance. As Catholics, when we have sinned we can not only tell someone but we can also be forgiven in the name of Jesus Christ.

In a pastoral letter for Advent 1998, Archbishop George Pell, at that time Archbishop of Melbourne, elaborated on this aspect of the sacrament: "It would be ironic in an age where we are encouraged to verbalise our problems, and speak about our concerns, when so many more people are helped by competent counsellors, psychologists and psychiatrists, that the personal exchanges necessary in individual confession to a priest should be falling into disuse. Many people are helped wonderfully in the First Rite of Penance, because the combination of personal confession, sincere repentance, absolution, advice and penance are the best means to deal with guilt." Indeed, it has often been said that many people would not need to have recourse to a counsellor or psychologist if they made more regular use of the Sacrament of Penance.

4. We need to know we are forgiven

Fourthly, we need to know that we are forgiven. We need to hear it in a human way. When we were children growing up, we did many wrong things. We went to our parents and told them we were sorry. If they just grunted and didn't reply, we wouldn't know whether we were forgiven and we would be very uneasy. But when they put their arms around us and said, "Don't worry, dear, I forgive you", we were at peace. As is obvious, the human need to know we have been forgiven is deeply rooted in human nature.

Of course, we can tell God directly that we are sorry, but then we don't hear that we are forgiven, and we might wonder whether we are sufficiently sorry and really determined to avoid committing that sin again. Moreover, we have probably had the experience of having sinned, sometimes even grievously, of saying an act of contrition with the intention of going to confession, and finding that the real peace did not come until we actually went to confession and heard the words, "I absolve you from your sins". We need to hear those words with our ears, and only then are we certain that we are forgiven. After all, we are human beings with a body and soul, not pure spirits, and Our Lord instituted the sacraments as outward signs precisely so that we could know when grace is acting in us.

In this way, through the mediation of the priest who absolves us, the Sacrament of Penance brings Christ close to the penitent. Pope John Paul II, speaking in a general audience on 22nd February 1984, asked the question, "Why should I reveal to a man like myself my most intimate situation, and even my most secret sins? Why can't I address myself directly to God, or to Christ, instead of having to go through the mediation of a man in order to obtain forgiveness for my sins?" He answered, "It is well to consider that despite the feeling of discomfort that ecclesial mediation can cause, it is a very human method, so that the God who frees us from our sins does not fade into a far off abstraction which would, in the end, become a colourless, irritating and despairing imitation of ourselves. Through the mediation of the Church's minister, this God makes himself very close to us in the concrete reality of a heart that is indeed pardoned. In this perspective we come to ask whether the Church's instrumentality, instead of being contested, should not rather be desired, since it responds to the deepest expectations that are hidden in the human soul, when one approaches God and lets himself be saved by him."

When we hear the words of absolution we *know* we are forgiven. Jesus, after all, instituted the sacrament in the form of a judgment: "Whose sins you shall forgive, they are forgiven. Whose sins you shall retain, they are retained." (*Jn* 20:23) The priest, having judged our understanding of what we have done and our degree of sorrow, determines that he can forgive us and he pronounces the words of absolution. Then "what is loosed on earth is loosed in heaven." (*Mt* 16:19) Without the mediation and judgment of the priest we would, in the end, be judging ourselves, and no one can be a good judge in his own case. We would always tend to let ourselves off the hook too lightly.

What is more, that encounter with Jesus Christ is, in a sense, a right of the penitent and a right of Christ as well. Pope John Paul II, in his very first encyclical *Redemptor hominis*, wrote: "In faithfully observing the centuries-old practice of the Sacrament of Penance, the practice of individual confession, with a personal act of sorrow and the intention to amend and make satisfaction, the Church is therefore defending the human soul's individual right. As is evident, this is also a right on Christ's part with regard to every human being redeemed by him. His right to meet each one of us in that key moment in the soul's life constituted by the moment of conversion, forgiveness." (RH 20)

Is this not the way Christ healed the sick and forgave sinners when he was on earth? He came close to them and laid hands on them one by one. As someone once commented to me facetiously, only on one occasion did Jesus heal ten lepers at once, and they were a most ungrateful lot! He wants to come close and lay his hands individually on each person, and therefore he institutes this sacrament. In this regard the use of the grille or screen can be helpful. Apart from allowing the penitent to remain anonymous, which is a right of every penitent, the fact that the penitent cannot see the priest makes it more clear that he or she is confessing not merely to the priest but to Christ himself.

The dedication of priests

Naturally, if Christ's intention of allowing each sinner to be absolved personally is to be made effective, it requires great dedication on the part of priests. As is well known, the history of the Church is filled with heroic examples of priests spending long hours, year after year in the confessional. The extraordinary witness of such priests as the Curé of Ars and Padre Pio springs immediately to mind. But far more common are the countless unacclaimed pastors all over the world who are only too willing to hear the confessions of their people whenever required.

One such example is that of an auxiliary bishop from the diocese of Huancavelica, high in the Andes of Peru, with whom I spoke some years ago. There were 335,000 Catholics in his diocese, looked after by only 20 priests, 16 of whom were over the age of 65. The bishop told about visiting a particular village to which he could go only once or twice a year. To reach the village he travelled seven hours by car, followed by six more on horseback. On arrival he heard confessions for two hours, then celebrated Mass and reserved the Blessed Sacrament. Afterwards he heard confessions for four more hours or longer until all the confessions were heard.

He mentioned that the 71 year-old diocesan bishop heard some 1,000 confessions a week. He would sometimes enter a church at 8pm and leave at 7am, having heard confessions, confirmed and married people all night. I asked the bishop if he ever gave general absolution, and he answered simply: "No, there is no need." He was a true minister of Jesus Christ, willing to sacrifice his own comfort so that each soul could have a personal encounter with the divine Master.

Moreover, this willingness to hear confessions individually testifies to the dignity and value of each person. Pope John Paul II, in an address to Mexican bishops some years ago, said: "The very poorest, as are many of the members of your diocese, for whom nobody takes time in our restless and hurried society, can give witness, if they are received by the priest with love and respect in the Sacrament of Penance, to the fact that the Church welcomes everyone, respects and listens to everyone, with that personal love which expresses itself in the care and affection of Christ for each and every one whom he has redeemed by his Blood. In the exercise of the ministry of the confessional, the priest who makes himself readily available for each of the faithful who needs his service, is the visible witness of the dignity of each one of the baptised."

The benefits of Confession

The Sacrament of Penance not only responds to deep human needs, it is also a source of many blessings.

Forgiveness of our sins

First of all, and most importantly, we receive forgiveness of our sins. We have sinned against the infinite majesty and love of God, and by ourselves we would have no way of making up. But, like the prodigal son, we go before our Father God in all humility and beg him to forgive us. We do not have to wait long to hear the words of absolution. Commenting on the difference between human tribunals and the tribunal of God, a 20th century champion of the Sacrament of Penance, St Josemaria Escriva, writes in his popular book *The Way*, "What depths of mercy there are in God's justice! For, in the judgments of men, he who confesses his fault is punished; and in the judgment of God, he is pardoned." (TW 309) This sacrament is truly, in the words of St Josemaria, "a miracle of God's love".

Growth in self-knowledge

But even before we confess our sins we have to examine our conscience, and that act of looking at our life and seeing how we have failed to respond to God's love for us is very helpful. It helps us to get to know ourselves, to see where we have failed since our last confession and where we repeatedly fail. It thus gives us growth in self-knowledge which, as a means to spiritual growth, to amendment of life, to struggling harder to improve, is a great help.

Humility

The examination of conscience, together with the act of confessing our sins, helps us to grow in humility, in the truth about how we really are, including our faults. We all tend to have an exaggerated sense of our self worth and a diminished realisation of our defects. St Teresa of Avila says that "the devil has as his chief mission to make us proud", and he succeeds much of the time. Then let us go to confession frequently so that we can grow in humility and come to the awareness of our true worth.

Sincerity

Also, in confession we grow in sincerity or truthfulness. In confessing our sins we cannot beat around the bush – we have to be clear. To acknowledge to ourselves and then to tell the priest in clear terms what we have done, is an exercise of and a means of growth in sincerity. Obviously we don't have to mention all the minute details, but when the sin is mortal we must at least mention the type and the number of times we have committed the sin. Our experience in being sincere with

God in confession can make it easier afterwards to be more sincere with others.

Sanctifying grace

Another great fruit of confession is of course sanctifying grace, that habitual grace which is a sharing in God's own life and which, as its very name suggests, sanctifies us and makes us pleasing to God. We are all called to be saints, and we are sanctified by God's life within us. I once came to realise the importance of confession as a means of receiving sanctifying grace while visiting a woman in hospital. I was wondering what I could do for her, besides giving her conversation and a blessing, since on that occasion I could not take her Holy Communion. But then I remembered that I could give her a sacrament, the Sacrament of Penance, and with it an increase of sanctifying grace. I asked her if she would like to go to confession, and she said yes. If it were only for the sanctifying grace we would have ample reason to go to confession frequently.

Actual grace

In addition to sanctifying grace, we receive actual grace, the passing help of God to do good deeds and avoid committing sin. The actual grace, or sacramental grace, given in this Sacrament is the special help to avoid committing in the future the sins we have just confessed. It is not that we will be able to avoid them completely –

after all, we are not perfect – but we receive the help of grace to be stronger in struggling against them. This is not only a theory but the experience of anyone who goes regularly to confession. After we have confessed something, we are much more successful in avoiding falling again into the same sins.

Strength in the spiritual struggle

Helped by this sacramental grace, confession gives us a new beginning in the spiritual struggle. Perhaps we have confessed only venial sins, but the soul, which had been "stained" with the guilt and habit of those sins, is now cleansed and purified of the guilt. This affords a great incentive to struggle harder to keep the soul pure. It is a bit like taking a shower and putting on clean clothes after we have been working in the garden. Once clean, we want to stay that way. After confession we always do better. And the more often we go to confession, the more often we renew our struggle and the more quickly we advance along the way of holiness.

In this regard Pope Benedict XVI explained in his General Audience on the 12th April 2006 that the Sacrament of Penance is "a kind of death and resurrection for each one of us." He went on to say that "it offers us the possibility to begin our life again and this new beginning is realised in the joy of the Risen One and in the communion of forgiveness that it gives us."

Spiritual direction

Then too, through confession we receive spiritual direction. Most priests offer at least a few words of encouragement, of advice, of clarification of conscience about what the penitent has just confessed. It may be only a brief encounter but it can be very helpful in the spiritual life. For many people, the occasion of confession is their regular opportunity to receive a deeper spiritual direction.

In this regard Pope John Paul II said in his general audience on 11th April 1984: "Certainly, 'spiritual direction' (or 'spiritual counsel', or 'spiritual dialogue', as some prefer to express it at times) can be carried out even outside the context of the Sacrament of Penance and even by someone who is not endowed with Holy Orders. However, it cannot be denied that this function – insufficient, if it is done only within a group, without a personal relationship – is in fact frequently and happily linked to the Sacrament of Reconciliation and is done by a 'teacher' of life (cf *Eph* 4:11), by a *'spiritualis senior'* (spiritual elder) (*Rule of St Benedict*, chap. 4, 50-51), by a 'doctor' (cf. *Summa Theologiae, Supplementum*, q. 18), by a 'guide in the things of God' (*ibid.*, q. 36, a. 1) who is the priest, who is made suitable for special duties 'in the Church' by a 'singular gift of grace' (*ibid.*, q. 35, a. 1). In this way the penitent overcomes the danger of arbitrariness and is helped to know and to decide his vocation in the light of God."

It is not easy to admit to another human being what we have done, especially when the priest knows us. But isn't this confession to one who knows us, humbling though it may be, rather something to be desired? When we take our car to be serviced, do we go to a different mechanic each time so that no one gets to know the car? And when we go to a doctor, do we go to a different one each time? No, we go to a doctor who knows us, and a mechanic who knows our car, precisely because they do know us and will thus be in a better position to apply the appropriate remedy. If we are consistent, we should not act any differently as regards our soul, which is far more important than our bodily health or our car.

Penance

Another benefit offered by confession is the penance which the priest asks us to undertake. As we know, every sin harms the mystical body of Christ and the sinner must make up in some measure for the harm caused. This is known as temporal punishment, and it must be undergone either here on earth through good deeds, penances or indulgences, or in Purgatory. Left to our own devices we might be inclined to do too little penance, but the penance which the priest proposes makes up at least in some measure for the temporal punishment owing for our sins. Assuredly, those who go regularly to confession may have to spend a much shorter time in Purgatory.

Reconciliation with the Church

Related to the penance which helps to make up for some of the temporal punishment is the reconciliation with the Church brought about by the sacrament, through the mediation of the Church's minister, the priest. As all members of the Church are one in the body of Christ, every sin harms the mystical body, just as every good deed contributes to the spiritual welfare of the Church. Through confession we are reconciled not only with God but also with the Church and forgiven for the harm we have caused. This is more obviously the case when we are forgiven for mortal sins, which cut us off from communion with God and the Church altogether.

Healing of the person

Another very important benefit of confession, one never to be underestimated, is the healing of the person from such attitudes as bitterness, anger, hatred, desire for revenge, sadness, and even depression. How often people have found that only after a good confession were they truly healed and restored to their customary serenity and charitableness. No amount of psychotherapy or counselling can ever achieve the inner healing that this sacrament brings about by destroying sin at its root.

Joy and peace

And finally, as the fruit of all we have mentioned, confession invariably gives great joy and peace of soul, through the knowledge that we are forgiven and that the burden that was weighing on us has been lifted. The experience of many people is that this is one of the greatest joys they have ever had, especially when the sins were mortal and thus severed their covenantal relationship with their Father God. This joy is symbolised by the joy of the prodigal son on being welcomed back by his father, the example Christ gives as an image of the sinner returning to the grace of God the Father. (cf *Lk* 15:11ff.)

In this regard Pope Benedict XVI said in an address on 19th February 2007: "How many penitents find the peace and joy in confession that they have been pursuing for a long time! How can we not acknowledge that also in our time, marked by so many religious and social challenges, this sacrament must be rediscovered and proposed again."

The frequency of Confession

If confession offers so many benefits, and if Christ gave this sacrament to the Church as a gift, it is only natural that we should want to take advantage of it often. We need it and it will give us the vitality, the self-knowledge, the humility, the sincerity, the grace, etc., that we need to be truly effective leaven, salt and light in society.

How often?

How often should we go to confession? Obviously there can be times in life when we *must* go. This is especially the case when one has committed a mortal sin, which ruptures communion with God and, unless it is repented of, prevents the person from going to heaven. It is true that sincere contrition moved by the sorrow of having offended God who is all good and worthy of our love restores the soul to the state of grace, but only if it is accompanied by the intention of going to confession. As the *Catechism of the Catholic Church* says, perfect contrition, arising from a love by which God is loved above all else, "obtains forgiveness of mortal sins if it includes the firm resolution to have recourse to sacramental confession as soon as possible." (CCC 1452) Just as a person who has broken a leg seeks out a doctor as soon as possible, so the sinner who has broken his relationship with God will seek to be reconciled with him immediately.

And of course one cannot receive Holy Communion after mortal sin without first going to sacramental confession. This traditional teaching is stated clearly in the *Catechism*: "Anyone aware of having sinned mortally must not receive Communion without having received absolution in the Sacrament of Penance." (CCC 1415) Anyone can commit a mortal sin, but we should have the honesty and love for God to confess that sin sacramentally before going to receive Holy Communion.

We should not forget either that "children must go to the Sacrament of Penance before receiving Holy Communion for the first time." (CCC 1457)

Then too, the obligation of confessing serious sins at least once a year remains in force: "After having attained the age of discretion, each of the faithful is bound by an obligation faithfully to confess serious sins at least once a year." (CCC 1457) But this is obviously establishing only a minimum requirement. Anyone wanting to grow in love for God will take advantage of confession on a regular basis.

Widely encouraged

The Magisterium of the Church has always encouraged frequent confession. One of the most often quoted passages is that of Pope Pius XII in his Encyclical *Mystici*

Corporis, where the Pope attributes the introduction of the practice of frequent confession to the Holy Spirit: "For a constant and speedy advancement in the path of virtue we highly recommend the pious practice of frequent confession, introduced by the Church under the guidance of the Holy Spirit; for by this means we grow in a true knowledge of ourselves and in Christian humility, bad habits are uprooted, spiritual negligence and apathy are prevented, the conscience is purified and the will strengthened, salutary spiritual direction is obtained, and grace is increased by the efficacy of the sacrament itself. Therefore those among the young clergy who are diminishing esteem for frequent confession, are to know that the enterprise upon which they have embarked is alien to the Spirit of Christ and most detrimental to the mystical Body of our Saviour."

The encouragement of frequent confession was reiterated by the Sacred Congregation for the Doctrine of the Faith in its 1972 *Pastoral Norms Concerning the Administration of General Sacramental Absolution*: "Priests should be careful not to discourage the faithful from frequent or devotional confession. On the contrary, let them draw attention to its fruitfulness for Christian living (cf *Mystici Corporis*) and always display readiness to hear such a confession whenever a reasonable request is made by the faithful. It must be absolutely prevented that individual confession should be reserved for serious sins only, for this would deprive the faithful of the great benefit of confession and would injure the good name of those who approach the sacrament singly."

And Pope John Paul II, in an address to priests at the beginning of Lent in 1981, said: "The sphere of the use of the Sacrament of Reconciliation cannot be reduced to the mere hypothesis of grave sins; apart from the considerations of a dogmatic character that could be made in this connection, we recall that confession periodically renewed, the so-called confession 'of devotion', has always accompanied the ascent to holiness in the Church."

On 27th March 2004 he said: "It would be an illusion to want to strive for holiness in accordance with the vocation that God has given to each one of us without frequently and fervently receiving this sacrament of conversion and sanctification." Confession is a powerful means of growing in holiness and if we take our calling to holiness seriously we will make frequent use of confession.

In view of this criterion, monthly, fortnightly or even weekly confession is much to be desired. It should be recalled that in order to gain plenary indulgences – and the Church makes them so readily available – one must go to the Sacrament of Penance some days before or after gaining the indulgence.

Blessed Pope John XXIII gives us his own example in encouraging frequent confession. At the age of 80 he wrote a note which would later be included in his *Journal of a Soul*: "During my whole life I have kept faithful to my practice of weekly confession. Several times during my life I have renewed my general confession."

Benefits

Someone might argue that there is little point in going to confession frequently when we are only going to go out and fall into the same sins again anyway. But we wash our bodies frequently when we are only going to get dirty again, and we eat regularly when we are only going to get hungry again. At least it is good to be clean some of the time, and with our appetite satisfied some of the time! Of course, for our sorrow to be genuine, we must be determined to struggle to avoid falling again into the same sins, even though we know by experience that we may not succeed.

Given the great benefit of confession to those who make use of it, it is not surprising that the devil does everything in his power to discourage people from taking advantage of it. Unfortunately he has been very successful in recent times. The following words are very relevant to the present situation: "Most holy persons are firmly persuaded that whatever of piety, of holiness, or religion, has been preserved to our times in the Church, through God's goodness, must be ascribed in great measure to confession. It cannot, therefore, be a matter of surprise that the enemy of the human race, in his efforts to destroy utterly the Catholic Church, should, through the agency of his wicked designs, have assailed with all his might this bulwark, as it were, of Christian virtue." Those words, while very applicable to the situation we have been witnessing in the past decades, were in fact written over 400 years ago, in the *Catechism for Parish Priests* issued after the Council of Trent.

Helping others to go to Confession

It is not enough simply to go to confession frequently ourselves. We should make a great effort to help others to go as well. We cannot forget that episode in the fifth chapter of St Luke's Gospel, where the friends of a paralytic brought their friend to Jesus. He could not walk, and had to be carried on a stretcher. They could not get into the house because of the large number of people, so they went up onto the roof and lowered him down in the midst of the assembly. What did Jesus say? "Rise up and walk", as everyone would have expected? No, "Your sins are forgiven". He gave that man the greatest blessing in his power. Even greater than curing his physical paralysis was healing the paralysis of his soul. Afterwards of course Jesus did heal the man's physical paralysis in order to show that he had the power to forgive sins. We should not forget that the paralytic was forgiven and healed because his friends took him to Jesus. Around us there are many people who are spiritually paralysed and who will not think of going to confession unless someone helps them.

Love and joy

Just as we invite others to read a book we have liked or to see a film we have seen, it would be only natural to do the same when it is a matter of the spiritual and human welfare of our relatives and friends. We all have acquaintances who have not been to confession for a long time and we would be showing little real concern or love for them if we did not speak to them about something as important as confession. If we do succeed in getting them back to confession we will be giving them, as well as ourselves, the great joy of coming closer to God.

The following anecdote, this one again from Peru, is one of the countless which could be related to exemplify this truth. A priest was just leaving the confessional when a man came and asked if he could hear his confession. The priest explained that he had been called to attend to a dying man but would return shortly. After about a half hour he returned and heard the man's confession. The man then explained that he had brought a friend who had not been to confession for some 40 years, and he urged the priest to treat his friend kindly lest he become frightened and never return. The priest heard the friend's confession as well as that of his wife and several others. When he left the confessional he met the man and his wife, who was holding an infant crying inconsolably. "Is the baby sick?" he asked. They told the priest that they had just walked for two days over the mountains to find a priest, since there were no priests in their own village. They had no money and during those days they had had nothing to eat, so that the woman had nothing with which to feed the baby. The priest, naturally, arranged food and lodging for the visitors.

The story illustrates the great value some people place on confession and the effort they are prepared to make to take advantage of it. It is one of the great treasures we have in the Catholic Church. In this country, where confession is readily available, perhaps we are inclined to take it too much for granted.

Some non-Catholics envy us for this sacrament. I was told recently about a man who was showing his non-Catholic wife around the cathedral in Washington, D.C. It was not a Sunday and there were several benches full of people in one part of the cathedral. The wife asked what those people were doing, and her husband explained that they were going to confession. He continued showing her around and at one point he noticed that she had disappeared. Some time later she reappeared and when he asked where she had been, she explained: "I went to confession!"

Recourse to Mary, refuge of sinners

If we want extra help to convince our friends to go to confession, I suggest we go to Our Lady. She stood beside the Cross while Our Lord gave his life to win for us the grace of salvation and, as Mother of the Redeemer and Refuge of Sinners, she will be eager to lead souls to her Son so that they can obtain that grace. My experience over many years hearing confessions in St Mary's Cathedral in Sydney, an experience which I later learned Cardinal Freeman also had, was that around feast days of Our Lady there were invariably more people in confession and more people for whom their confession was especially significant. I sometimes asked them why they had come and seldom did anyone make reference to the feast, of which they were obviously unaware. I was convinced that it was Our Lady herself who was bringing them back to Jesus.

Mending our ways

Pope John Paul II, in a homily in the Basilica of Our Lady of Zapopan in Mexico in the first year of his pontificate, encouraged us to have recourse to Mary in this apostolate: "She is refuge of sinners... If we are oppressed by awareness of sin, we instinctively seek him who has the power to forgive sins (cf. *Lk* 5:24), and we seek him through Mary, whose sanctuaries are places of conversion, penance and reconciliation with God. She awakens in us the hope of mending our ways and persevering in good, even if that may sometimes seem humanly impossible. She enables us to overcome the multiple 'structures of sin' in which our personal, family and social life is wrapped. She enables us to obtain the grace of true liberation, with that freedom with which Christ liberated every man."

Examination of Conscience

LOVE OF GOD

First Commandment: I am the Lord your God. You shall not have strange gods before me

Have I neglected my spiritual life?

Have I deliberately refused to believe a truth taught by the Church?

Have I sought to bring undue glory, recognition or credit to myself at the expense of the glory due to God?

Have I been involved in séances, used ouija boards, tarot cards or engaged in any other occult or satanic practices?

Have I put my trust in horoscopes, good luck charms, fortune tellers, palm readers, etc.?

Have I worshipped regularly in a non-Catholic or non-Christian church?

Have I received Communion in a state of mortal sin?

Have I deliberately told a lie or withheld a mortal sin in confession?

Second Commandment: You shall not take the Name of the Lord your God in vain

Have I used the name of God, Jesus, Christ, Mary, or the saints in a disrespectful way?

Have I deliberately harboured hatred, anger or resentment against God?

Have I wished evil on another person or cursed them?

Have I lied under oath or violated a vow?

Have I harmed a sacred person – a priest or religious – or abused a sacred object?

Have I failed to stand up for the Catholic faith when it was attacked?

Third Commandment: Remember to keep holy the Lord's Day

Have I deliberately missed Mass without a serious reason on a Sunday or Holy Day of Obligation?

Have I habitually arrived late for Mass or left early without good reason?

Have I failed to pay proper attention during Mass?

Have I failed to observe the proper rest and dedication to my family on Sundays?

Have I done unnecessary shopping or work on Sundays?

Have I failed to observe the Eucharistic fast of one hour before Communion?

Have I deliberately failed to fast or abstain from meat on Ash Wednesday or Good Friday?

LOVE OF NEIGHBOUR

Fourth Commandment:
Honour your father and mother

Have I failed to love, honour or respect my parents?

Have I failed to care properly for my aged or sick parents?

Have I failed to show the respect due to all people of advanced age?

Have I neglected my duties towards my spouse and children?

Have I failed to baptise my children in a reasonable time (within a few weeks or months of birth)?

Have I neglected to give my children proper religious instruction?

Fifth Commandment: You shall not kill

Have I harboured anger, resentment or ill will?

Have I been uncharitable in my dealings with others: arguing strongly, fighting, speaking unkindly?

Have I physically harmed anyone?

Have I harboured hatred or ill will towards persons because of their race or religion?

Have I failed to respect and uphold the dignity of every human person, no matter what their age or condition?

Have I abused alcohol or drugs or encouraged others to?

Have I driven a vehicle under the influence of drugs or alcohol or driven recklessly?

Have I failed to take proper care of my health by working too hard, not getting adequate rest, not eating the proper food, not taking prescribed medicines, etc.?

Have I given scandal by leading others into sin?

Have I placed myself without good reason in situations that might easily lead me into sin – relationships, readings, lectures, conversations, films, internet sites, etc.?

Have I surgically or chemically sterilised my reproductive capacity in order to avoid conceiving a child, or have I encouraged others to do so?

Have I had an abortion, participated in one, or encouraged another to do so?

Have I seriously considered or attempted suicide?

Have I participated in euthanasia by deliberately hastening or causing the death of a suffering person?

Sixth Commandment:
You shall not commit adultery

Have I engaged in passionate kissing or touching with another person outside marriage?

Have I committed impure acts by myself (masturbation), with another unmarried person (fornication), with a married person (adultery) or with someone of the same sex (homosexual acts)?

Have I been flirtatious with people other than my spouse?
Have I used or encouraged others to use contraception?
Have I interrupted the marriage act in such a way that the seed was spilled outside my wife's body?
Have I refused the marriage act without good reason?
Have I pressured my spouse into the marriage act without due sensitivity?
Have I been an occasion of sin to others through immodesty in my dress, conversation or behaviour?
Have I shared a house or a room with my boyfriend or girlfriend, thus putting myself in an occasion of sin?

Seventh Commandment: You shall not steal

Have I stolen anything or cooperated in other's stealing – e.g. by approving or encouraging them, or by receiving stolen goods?
Have I destroyed or damaged the property of others, including public property?
Have I failed to make restitution for any stolen or damaged property? If so, am I now prepared to make restitution insofar as I am able?
Have I gambled excessively?
Have I failed to work hard and to live justice with my employer or employees?
Have I been dishonest in my tax affairs?

Have I travelled on public transport without paying the proper fare?

Have I copied software or recordings without paying the proper fee?

Have I spent money extravagantly or wastefully?

Have I failed to help the disadvantaged when I had an opportunity to do so?

Eighth Commandment: You shall not bear false witness against your neighbour

Have I told lies or exaggerated the truth?

Have I gossiped about the faults of others?

Have I failed to defend those unjustly criticised?

Have I revealed the hidden faults of others without good reason?

Have I lied about others and damaged their reputation?

Have I revealed secrets or violated the confidence of others without good reason?

Ninth Commandment: You shall not desire your neighbour's wife

Have I deliberately taken pleasure in impure pictures, articles, books, films or internet sites?

Have I looked at others in an impure way?

Have I deliberately taken pleasure in impure memories, imaginations or desires?

Have I wilfully lusted after another?

Tenth Commandment: You shall not desire your neighbour's goods

Have I envied others for their material possessions?

Am I excessively attached to material goods?

Have I desired or planned to steal, destroy or damage the property of another?

Have I failed to trust that God will take care of me in my material needs?

Have I failed to be grateful to God for all he has given me?

The Rite of Confession

The penitent begins by making the sign of the Cross:
In the name of the Father and of the Son and of the Holy Spirit. Amen.

Invitation

The priest then invites the penitent to make a good confession in these or similar words:
May the Lord be in your heart and help you to confess your sins with true sorrow, to which the penitent answers *Amen.*

Scripture

Either the penitent or the priest may then read or recite from memory some brief text of Scripture that proclaims God's mercy and calls man to conversion.

Confession

The penitent then makes his/her confession, telling the priest how long it has been since the last confession and mentioning any mortal sins committed since the last confession with the number of times those sins have been committed, and also any venial sins they may wish to confess.

Penance

The priest gives whatever advice or encouragement he deems fitting and then invites the penitent to do some act of penance, which the penitent should do as soon as possible after the confession.

Contrition

The priest then asks the penitent to express his/her sorrow, which the penitent may do with a brief aspiration such as *Lord Jesus, Son of God, have mercy on me, a sinner* or a longer act of contrition such as:

My God, I am sorry for my sins with all my heart. In choosing to do wrong and failing to do good, I have sinned against you, whom I should love above all things. I firmly intend, with your help, to do penance, to sin no more, and to avoid whatever leads me to sin. Our Saviour Jesus Christ suffered and died for us. In his name, my God, have mercy.

Absolution

The priest, extending his hands over the penitent, then gives the absolution, saying:

God the Father of mercies, through the death and resurrection of his Son has reconciled the world to himself and sent the Holy Spirit among us for the forgiveness of sins; through the ministry of the Church may God give you pardon and peace, and I absolve you from your sins in the name of the Father and of the Son and of the Holy Spirit.

The penitent answers: *Amen.*

Conclusion

The priest may continue with a prayer such as:

The Lord has freed you from your sins. Go in peace.
The penitent answers: *Thanks be to God.*

Or the priest may say:

May the Passion of our Lord Jesus Christ, the intercession of the Blessed Virgin Mary, and of all the saints, whatever good you do and suffering you endure, heal your sins, help you to grow in holiness, and reward you with eternal life. Go in peace.

LIGHTHOUSE TALKS

CAN YOU TRUST GOD?
DR. TIM GRAY

Dr. Gray addresses the pervasi
misconceptions that God is qu
to anger, that the God of the
Old and New Testaments are
different, and that God doesn'
have a merciful heart for us.

MEN AND WOMEN ARE FROM EDEN
DR. MARY HEALY

With incredible clarity, Dr. He
explains how the *Theology of th
Body* is astonishingly good nev
for a culture littered with brok
marriages, immorality, hearta
and loneliness.

DISCOVER WHY LIGHTHOUSE TALKS HAVE REACHED
MORE THAN 15 MILLION LISTENERS ACROSS THE GLOB

AUGUSTINE
INSTITUTE

To learn more, visit us at
augustineinstitute.org/audio
or call (866) 767-3155

FØRMED® THE CATHOLIC FAITH. ON DEMAND.

Discover the site that gathers more Catholic content in one place.

One convenient website
Save the time you used to spend searching and find the Catholic content you want. On demand and available when you are.

High quality
You'll always find beautiful, trustworthy, Catholic content.

New and updated regularly
Discover new and fresh materials every week.

ore choices
Easily choose from a wide range of content options: movies, Ebooks, audio talks, and video studies.

Login to formed.org for a free 7-day trial.